Contents

Other Books in Series	v
A Great Offer	vii
Introduction	xi
1. What is Astral Projection?	1
2. The Benefits of Astral Projection	7
3. The Risks of Astral Projection	15
4. Astral Projection Techniques	19
5. Developing The Right State of Mind	29
6. Influencing Your Astral Body	35
Conclusion	39
References	41
More Books by Monique	43
Last Chance	45
Thank You!	47

Other Books in Series

Personal and Self Development
Creative Visualization
Meditation for Beginners
Reiki for Beginners
Manifesting With the Law of Attraction
Stress Management
Time Bound
Healing Animals with Reiki
Being an Empath Today

Personal Growth and Development

ASTRAL PROJECTION FOR BEGINNERS

MONIQUE JOINER SIEDLAK

Oshun Publications

Astral Projection for Beginners © Copyright 2016 by Monique Joiner Siedlak

ISBN: 978-1-948834-44-5

All rights reserved

The content contained within this book may not be reproduced, duplicated or transmitted without direct written permission from the author or the publisher.

Under no circumstances will any blame or legal responsibility be held against the publisher, or author, for any damages, reparation, or monetary loss due to the information contained within this book, either directly or indirectly.

Legal Notice

This book is copyright protected. It is only for personal use. You cannot amend, distribute, sell, use, quote or paraphrase any part, or the content within this book, without the consent of the author or publisher.

Disclaimer Notice

Please note the information contained within this document is for educational and entertainment purposes only. All effort has been executed to present accurate, up to date, reliable, complete information. No warranties of any kind are declared or implied. Readers acknowledge that the author is not engaged in the rendering of legal, financial, medical or professional advice. The content within this book has been derived from various sources. Please consult a licensed professional before attempting any techniques outlined in this book.

By reading this document, the reader agrees that under no circumstances is the author responsible for any losses, direct or indirect, that are incurred as a result of the use of the information contained within this document, including, but not limited to, errors, omissions, or inaccuracies.

Cover Design by MJS

Cover Image by Lightworker and nordenworks@depositphotos.com

Published by Oshun Publications

www.oshunpublications.com

Want to learn about African Magic, Wicca, or even Reiki while cleaning your home, exercising, or driving to work? I know it's tough these days to simply find the time to relax and curl up with a good book. This is why I'm delighted to share that I have books available in audiobook format.

Best of all, you can get the audiobook version of this book or any other book by me for free as part of a 30-day Audible trial.

Members get free audiobooks every month and exclusive discounts. It's an excellent way to explore and determine if audiobook learning works for you.

If you're not satisfied, you can cancel anytime within the trial period. You won't be charged, and you can still keep your book. To choose your free audiobook, visit:

www.mojosiedlak.com/free-audiobooks

Introduction

When we look at ourselves in the mirror, we see an imperfect human being. A past riddled with so-called mistakes. We cannot seem to control an ever-changing future, and the existential dread of mortality creeping closer, resting its hand on our shoulder.

And that is all before we even drink our first cup of coffee in the morning.

When thinking of astral projection, many people immediately think of how it has been presented in popular films and television shows, which is not always accurate. Sometimes they do get it right and portray it as accurately as possible. However, the meaning behind it is left out, painting a bleak and colorless image of what astral travel and projection really is.

This book will discuss what astral projection really is, not merely skimming over the details, leaving you with more questions than what you had before starting this book.

Well, that is not entirely true, I suppose. Yes, after reading this book, your questions regarding astral travel will be answered sufficiently, leaving you with more knowledge than what you came here with. But, knowledge craves knowledge, and when someone learns something new, they want to apply that knowledge to everyday life. Think back to when you first started to absorb the infinite wisdom that is the subject of mathematics. You could not wait to gain more of it. That is until you began to realize that mathematics is not quite that simple. You most likely became discouraged, while some became more intrigued.

This is most likely due to the teacher, or even simply because you are not as interested as that one smart kid who seemed to be a math whiz. However, one of the main reasons we act this way is simply because we are inherently very narrow-minded when approaching a new subject, curious maybe. Still, we are terrified of something contradicting that which we believe to be the truth or absolute. This is not your fault. We are raised to think of a specific set of rules and regulations popularly known as "that's life."

We have been raised with preconceived ideas of what life is supposed to be, ideas passed down from parent to child, from media to consumer, from religion to follower. Taking a step back from normal life can sometimes provide you with the perspective needed for dealing with everyday problems you might be facing or answering questions you could not find the answer to from the daily walk of normal life.

This is why I will ask you now to have an open mind, not just when reading this book, but when dealing with any new subject matter, you might be presented with in the future. I am not asking you to completely disregard all you have been taught through life and blindly believe in what you read, ending up disastrous in many scenarios. I am asking you to simply suspend your beliefs and/or teachings temporarily. When a new subject matter is presented to you, be it through debate or learning materials, it will help you gain a new perspective more easily.

This advice is not to be taken lightly. It might help you learn something new in your future endeavors, instead of

Introduction

merely turning away at the thought of something you have difficulty understanding.

When approaching the subject of astral projection with an open mind, what you learn will open the door to a mystery you may or may not yet be aware of. The question many of us have lingering in the back of our minds, what is the true difference between mortality and immortality.

Rest easy knowing you will have your questions surrounding astral projection answered. However, know that your questions surrounding reality will expand. You seek more and more answers to what life is truly about once you start.

ONE

What is Astral Projection?

IF YOU ARE ENTIRELY NEW TO THIS SUBJECT, DON'T WORRY! We will be going over what precisely astral projection is, the history and origin, how people have perceived it throughout time, and what people think about it today. Some people do not believe it to be a truthful practice. In contrast, others commit their lives to it in a ritualistic manner. We will be looking at astral projection objectively, keeping our minds open to any possible meaning and use. Many people forget to disregard their personal opinions and feelings when looking into something new.

The biggest question I want you to ask yourself when you are finished reading this chapter is the most important question anyone can ask themselves: What if?

The Basics

Let's start off by discussing what astral projection actually is, or as many might recognize it by the term out-of-body-experience (OBE). Now first off, astral projection and OBEs are not the same things, strictly speaking, although they can be seen as similar.

Have you ever had a dream where you are seemingly floating, effortlessly moving around with your body visible in front of you? Or even found yourself in a strangely familiar environment, yet distant from where you fell asleep, just to be yanked back and feel your body jerking you awake.

It felt so real that you can swear it was.

The chances that you just had an OBE are quite promising. Your consciousness seems to have leaked out into reality itself, dancing around in the world without any constraints or limitations, no more strings attached to it.

How is this different from astral projection? Well, at its core, an OBE is accidental; it can occur without warning to anyone at any time, usually not lasting more than a few seconds. An OBE is also identified by the scientific/medical community, where many studies have been performed.

On the other hand, astral projection is the willful intent to project one's consciousness outward from your body. Lift your hand and look at it. Did you just lift your hand? Or did your brain tell your body to lift it? Is there even a difference.

In the end, if you really think about it, your body is a sort of shell which your brain is using to pilot around the world, walking around and communicating with others. It is the control center, the cockpit, and you are the consciousness inside making those decisions willfully. Consciousness is believed to be a part of the brain, but what if it is not physically connected to the brain.

The conscious part that makes you, you, can also be identified as the soul, spirit, inherent energy, or force, as believed by many different religions. So, in essence, astral projection is simply forcing that part of you out of your body, leaving your physical traits behind, seen by many as a spiritual practice. This is what separates astral projection from an OBE, projecting your spiritual energy outward rather than having it slip out while in a semi-conscious state.

This is where you need to separate your preconceived

ideas of reality from the now. Keep in mind that we have been raised to believe and trust in a certain way of thinking for hundreds of years; what if that way of understanding our reality is wrong.

For now, let's take a look at what information we have collected on this subject throughout history.

The History

The term astral projection was only coined in the 19th century. However, the idea of astral projection has been present in many cultures and religions around the world for hundreds of years and was most likely present before recorded history.

Looking at the many sides of history, astral projection has many interpretations throughout many religions and beliefs. We will place them in two groups, namely "Western" and "Eastern."

In Western culture, astral projection is mainly seen as a way to travel the astral planes between our physical realm, heaven, and then hell. The body and the soul are seen as two separate things connected via either chain, cord, or light. In this context, the astral plane can be described as an area populated by angels, demons, and spirits that can be entered and traversed willingly or accidentally. This is the most popular version of astral projection seen in mainstream media, usually portrayed with religious connections and intent. There are many layers to the Western belief system of astral projection. However, this is the most basic. We have our world or realm, the astral world or bridge, and then the higher realms connect to us via the astral bridge.

Some Western beliefs have been influenced by Eastern cultures. Many people have taken it upon themselves to explore different ideas and then translate those ideas to those who cannot understand that which is too different from their own beliefs. It is tough for Western cultures to understand the inherently "free" thinking of some Eastern religions, as western religions are usually more strict and refined.

Eastern culture, as with most of their religious beliefs, has a less strict and more open-minded idea around astral projection. The beliefs usually focus on the core energy of the body traditionally portrayed as spiritual energy. If appropriately used through meditation and focus, this energy can be harnessed to construct a spiritual body with which astral exploration may be conducted.

The soul or spirit in this belief system is usually not just a part of you but also a part of all the universe's energy. So to move around the all, one must focus your own consciousness into an astral body of sorts so that it may not become lost in the sea of reality when death comes for the physical body.

Many other beliefs are surrounding astral projection as well. In the Book of the Dead authored by the Egyptians years ago, they portray their understanding of what the individual might be constructed of. The body is our physical connection to the world, and the soul our eternal force, consisting of 5 or more parts.

Japanese mythology portrays the soul as something separate from the body; it can leave the body and appear in front of someone against which a great grudge is held to curse them.

These are simple and basic ideas and beliefs cultures have cultures that might seem completely different from each other on the surface. Due to our lack of understanding and fearfulness of something different from what we are accustomed to, most people have neglected to realize they are inherently the same.

It is important to note one thing. If anything from the information we have collected throughout history, all religions and beliefs have some semblance of the soul, spirit, or inner force/energy. This trait that our religions and beliefs share can usually be either harnessed or used to travel to a different reality or perceive reality as it truly is, without the physical body's constraints.

What Does It All Mean?

We are now familiar with how astral projection has been interpreted and portrayed through history, albeit small segments of history. It provides us with an overall understanding of the bigger picture that surrounds astral projection.

What should you do with this new information, and what does it mean? Well, those are two questions that you can answer only for yourself. As with many beliefs and religions, it all depends on the individual. Astral projection is a way to open a door that you usually cannot open or even see. This is because we are so stuck on the idea that the reality we perceive with our physical senses is by logic the only reality possible, which is simply not true.

I say this because there are things out there in our physical world which we cannot see, feel, hear or smell. We need equipment to monitor or understand it, ranging from different gases, wavelengths, particles, energies, and more. So the possibility that there are things in our perceived reality which we cannot fathom or even begin to comprehend without the proper equipment, knowledge, and method is quite substantial.

Astral projection is simply one of these methods, a tool to be used to further our understanding of what reality truly is, be it to look inward to expand our personal knowledge or to explore the vast universe in a way we physically cannot.

The meaning of astral projection may differ from person to person. Still, in this book, we will be looking at it from a spiritual aspect, a way for you to build on yourself, your beliefs, and your spiritual health. Using it as a tool to open your mind for new possibilities to seep through your individually constructed reality, changing your perspective on life for the better.

The meaning you derive from something newly gained may not be the meaning another has come to understand from it. No one can tell you what something means to you spiritually. You can simply be given the knowledge and the methods of implementing that knowledge. At this point, you will have to decide for yourself what it means to you.

TWO

The Benefits of Astral Projection
─────────────────────────────────

ONE OF THE MANY REASONS PEOPLE ENJOY READING IS TO GAIN extra knowledge. To experience that thrill of coming to understand something previously unthought-of and adding it to their mental library. Of course, some may only read for the pure enjoyment of reading, experiencing characters' emotions, or living another's life. Some will read simply for the beneficial knowledge it may bring them, and some for learning a new mandatory subject.

The reason you are reading this book might not be the same as another reader's, however that does not mean you all cannot gain something from it, right? Why don't we look at what you may benefit from understanding this spiritual practice without forcing you into a specific direction?

Life After Death

What does life after death mean to you? Did you grow up with a specific religion? Or did you grow up not believing in any form of life after death.

Life after death has many meanings, depending on your beliefs, of course. Egyptians believed that your heart was weighed after death to determine if you are worthy of their version of the afterlife. Christianity has a similar belief: you are judged after death and sent to either heaven or hell.

This is a rather frightening idea of the afterlife. If you genuinely think about it, you have only one chance, your life, to prove yourself worthy of an eternal and blissful afterlife. However, Buddhism looks at the afterlife a bit differently, distinguishing the afterlife in two main ways.

First is what they call "samsara", the cycle of rebirth through karma. Simply put, depending on your actions throughout your life, you may be reborn as either human or animal. Secondly is what they call "nirvana", the ultimate goal is to escape the cycle of rebirth and enter nirvana. At this point, you will not be reborn but rather see reality as it truly is.

Many people believe astral projection is a way to experience this true reality. Still, we will discuss that in a later chapter. However, when achieving astral projection, it can be seen as proof of life after death for that individual.

This is where your spiritual growth reaches its infancy. Before this, you were simply wondering, curious if there is life after death, and how to experience it, how to prove it to yourself. Now you can start to focus on your personal and spiritual growth. You have been exposed to a new reality. How do you deal with that information.

When confronted with something new, will you deny its existence? Or will you embrace it? This is a question you must ask yourself. By no means will the answer be an easy one to accept, whether you decide to accept what you experienced and expand on it or discard it and move forward with your life as if it never happened. Either way, your life will never be the same again.

If chosen to accept what you experienced and build on that foundation, then I applaud you. This is no easy feat, as many do not want their lives to change in such an abrupt manner. This is why it is not something to be taken lightly, as your spiritual growth will only expand from here.

If chosen to deny this new reality, then I applaud you as well. There is no greater meaning to oneself than standing steadfast in what you believe. It helps cement your personal growth for the future and will outline your character to others.

Beneficial for some, personal and spiritual growth can help in the long run of life, however, short it might seem.

Expand Your Awareness

What does being aware mean to you? Knowing your physical location in the world or understanding your place in the world? Perhaps you thought it out a bit more, and awareness to you means being aware of your own conscious decisions that make you, you. Expanding your awareness surrounding your spiritual and physical surroundings will have many beneficial qualities that you might find intriguing.

Perceptual awareness is one of the more interesting things we will be focusing on for now, but what exactly is it.

Perceptual awareness and perception, in neurology and psychology, are sort of the same thing. When information enters the brain, it gets processed and then perceived by you. You will be aware of that information. It is possible. However, that information might enter the brain through your sensory organs and be processed but will not be perceived by your conscious mind, thus leaving you unaware of what might transpire.

Astral projection helps to improve your perceptual awareness. As you focus on your most inner self, you become more aware of the reality surrounding you. Not just by using your physical senses but also by using your spiritual ones. This is something the monks in Tibet have been perfecting for years; they can reach a very high focus and perceptual awareness.

It is quite difficult in our daily lives, as we have many

distractions surrounding us, clouding our perception of reality. Astral projection is simply one of the methods we can use to block all distractions to further expand our perception of reality.

Perception is subjective, of course, as the reality surrounding you is your own. You perceive as you have grown up to perceive, so how do we expand on that? How do we improve our perception of others and the reality surrounding them? We increase our knowledge of reality, and that can be achieved through astral projection.

It is a difficult subject to understand, but when I say we increase our knowledge, I do not necessarily mean tangible knowledge, but rather a knowledge of the self. When astral projecting, you are in the same reality others are, without the influence of physical intervention. It is here where your knowledge of the world becomes apparent in a more profound way. Now, I am not saying you will become all-knowing. That is a rather arrogant way of looking at it. Instead, you will come to understand a specific part of the reality on which you can further build your knowledge physical world.

When looking at astral projection in this way, you might come to realize that life after death might just be the immortal tale many believe to be true. If it is possible to remove one's consciousness from the body and move around freely, is it not possible to survive without the body.

The first law of thermodynamics states that energy can be changed from one form to another but cannot be created or destroyed. Bringing new meaning to the Buddhist teachings of "samsara." You do not die, but your spirit/energy is recycled to provide life to something new. It does make sense, especially if you are more prone to a logical thought process. Hence, immortality is, in fact, something that can exist in our reality, and astral projection just might be the key to understanding it.

Are There Physical Benefits.

This is quite an interesting topic, as many people believe astral projection to be the door to spiritual improvement. Many believe it can have beneficial effects on the physical body as well. It is not too hard to believe either, as the spirit and the body are two separate things, yet they intertwine to form one person.

The physical body might be just the current vessel we possess to traverse this form of reality we perceive. Still, we can improve the function of it through intense focus and astral projection. Let's go back to "out-of-body-experience" or OBE. As we discussed, they are slightly different from astral projection, yet in essence, still the same thing, just less refined. Many people have discovered a great use for these OBEs through lucid dreaming, a dream state in which the dreamer knows they are dreaming.

Lucid dreams have long been a catalyst for OBEs, and many people will most likely have their first OBE through the use of lucid dreaming. Let's not go off on a tangent and instead focus on how this may benefit you, through sleep, of course.

The mind takes quite a toll on the body when in an idle state. The brain accounts for about 20% of your overall bodily energy usage in a day, which might not sound like much. Still, thinking about all the different organs and movements that require energy throughout the day, it does seem quite significant. So now you are left to sleep a substantial amount of time during your life. On average, a person will sleep 7 to 9 hours per day, which amounts to 277,760 hours of sleep in the average life span. That's a lot of time that could seemingly be used more productively.

You might now begin to see the full picture. If not, then not to worry. I will be explaining anyway! You're reading this to learn new things in the first place, aren't you?

So if lucid dreaming occurs when you are asleep and acts as a catalyst for OBEs, doesn't that mean we can get at least some hours back from our sleep cycle? If implemented correctly, then yes, absolutely!

Some athletes have admitted to learning lucid dreaming and how to induce an OBE for the simple objective of practicing certain movement sets and visualizing the game they might expect to be playing. Having the conscious feel of movement without actually moving your body ends in your body actually getting the rest it needs. Your muscle memory is improving, heightening your natural reflexes and responses, adapting your mental state to a winning form. Not only is your body resting and healing itself more efficiently during sleep, but you can consciously improve your reflexes, knowledge, and spiritual awareness while this is happening.

In reality, other things are impossible to do physically, but what if they can be unlocked through astral projection.

Psychic abilities have long been discussed amongst people interested in paranormal topics, spiritual topics, and alternative medicine. It is a topic dismissed by many yet embraced by some to the point of absolute belief. I am not here to tell you one from the other. I am simply here to inform you of how astral projection can increase your aptitude towards such abilities.

Firstly, what qualifies as a psychic ability? There is a wide range of abilities classified as psychic, from the ability to communicate with spirits as a medium to the art of dowsing, which is to locate underground water or mineral sources. When thinking about astral projection, most people only think about where the spirit leaves the body, but what this practice does is inherently more complex.

Think of a doorway. You do not know what is hidden behind it. However, many people have speculated, others have hypothesized, and many more have theorized. You wish to see what lies behind the door, but cannot possibly hope to comprehend with your current knowledge, so you start preparing yourself. Through astral projection, you have fashioned a sort of key to open the door with, but you still do not quite understand what you see behind it, and so you return again. This idea might help you understand what reality really is and how astral projection might help obtain the knowledge to manipulate reality itself. Which we have labeled as psychic abilities.

The more you visit that side of the door, the more you understand, and the easier it becomes to open the door and use what lies beyond it.

We are simply stuck inside a small portion of reality, trying to understand a vast universe from the inside of a box. With our ideas of reality preconceived, you need to use specific methods to break free from those ideas. In turn, you can ready yourself for what might come next in the cycle of what we perceive as life.

THREE

The Risks of Astral Projection

WITH ANYTHING IN LIFE, TRYING SOMETHING NEW USUALLY comes with a risk, be this a physical risk, mental, emotional, or spiritual one. But we cannot let risk define us. Otherwise, where would we be?

Astral projection might not seem too risky for some, as the idea centers around spirituality, which many struggle to attach a tangible risk to. However, when thinking about your spiritual self as being your true self, the risk becomes more apparent. As we have discussed, your body is just here to help you navigate the physical world, with your consciousness/spirit/energy making the actual decisions.

Losing Yourself

I remember a while back when I was still relatively new to my car, I went to a massive mall. This specific mall had a multilayered parking lot separate from the main building. So I went to park in the first available parking spot I could find. This was my first time here, and I did not pay much attention to the level I parked on, as I was in a hurry to get to the fun part of my excursion.

After what seemed like a full day of walking around and enjoying all that my new experience had to offer, I had to leave. I walked towards the parking building and realized that I never took note of what level I parked on. This was not a fun experience. As it turned out, there were five levels, and so I had to go through at least three of these levels until I was able to find my car, and this was after searching through the whole level!

This is a common occurrence in popular media's portrayal of astral projection, having difficulty finding your way back to your own body. This is, however, not a real occurrence when you try astral projection. You do not have to rely on your physical memory to get back to your body. Forgetting where it is will be like forgetting who you are entirely.

Many cultures and religions believe you are tied to your body via a powerful connection, most of the time referenced as a silver string or cord. This cord is not so much a physical, literal string as it is figurative. It is the only way we can describe it through our current knowledge to identify it with something we are accustomed to. There are, however, other risks that might influence your return to your physical vessel.

Throughout religion, there are always mentions of otherworldly beings, usually classified as either good or evil. The most commonly recognized being angels and demons. Once again, these are preconceived ideas of what these beings truly are. Now, of course, something that intends to harm you will try its utmost to do so. However, this is not a common occurrence.

As humans, we have adopted this belief system that the presence of goodness will inherently mean there is evil. While this is true in light and dark, it is not necessarily the truth in reality. We have people who do bad things, but they do not do these things because they are evil. They do them because it is what they either grew up to believe is how they should live. Due to other environmental circumstances, we simply gave it the label of evil or good. When traversing the astral planes, you might encounter many different things, but you are composed of energy. Energy cannot be destroyed nor created, only changed from one form to another.

This means that you may lose yourself. You identify as your individuality, should your flow of energy change, as there are many forms of energy. People today tend to take things too literally or at face value. Unfortunately, this is the world we live in. Still, it is not the reality out there.

Things are not always what they seem and can only be explained by the reality that the individual has grown accustomed to and the context they hold life. My life experience will not be the same as yours, and thus the meaning I derive from my experiences will differ vastly from yours.

That being said, there are other beings out there. We simply gave them names such as demon or angel, god or devil. Can they influence your journey?

Literally or Figuratively

Possession is a topic usually discussed with religious intent, which carries its own weight. It is, after all, a terrifying thought to be possessed by something or someone else. When astral projection takes place, you force your inner self out of your body into reality as it is. Leaving your physical self seemingly defenseless. It stands to reason that your body is free for the taking, should someone, or something, be around to occupy it.

This is true, in the sense that your body is now just lying there defenseless. Someone can easily walk in on you and slice your belly open. If you have traveled far away, you might not even realize it until it is too late. It is always a good idea to perform this spiritual practice safely, which you know is protected physically. As for the possession of your body, it is quite different. If you look at your ID, you are given a specific number that identifies you on the local governing system. You can think of your body the same way as that ID, the local governing system being reality.

When you exit your body, that number remains, and only someone with that number can enter it at that time. You will have to grant permission to any being that wishes to occupy your vessel, giving them that number, so to speak. This can happen accidentally. However, but very unlikely, it's similar to how you sign something without reading it. Giving permission to whoever holds the contract to use your personal information, or body in this case. In the end, however, it is still your body, so you can get it back by simply taking it.

Reality is full of inarticulate information that we can only understand after passing on to the next stage in our immortal life cycle. Yes, you read that right. This is just the beginning, our bodies merely the ambassadors of our true life in this universe.

So you have heard enough? Do you want to try astral projection? Or have you decided that it is not quite your idea of how to interpret reality.

There are many ways, of course, as this world of ours is not simply binary.

FOUR

Astral Projection Techniques

REACHING THE POINT OF NO RETURN HAS NEVER BEEN MORE close to you than now. It is quite a strange feeling starting out with these types of practices, especially if you never even considered them a possibility.

It will be difficult when starting out, and it will take time, patience, effort, dedication, and conviction. When I say time, I do mean that it can take years depending on person to person. Some people tend to experience OBEs early in life and have a specific aptitude for spiritual progression. In contrast, others find it very difficult to get to the point of relaxing their entire body and clearing their minds.

Monks from all over the world dedicate their entire life to learning certain rituals and forms to reach a higher level of focus when meditating. The end-goal being reaching enlightenment, but who has that kind of time anyway?

We will focus on specific techniques used by practitioners worldwide from different cultures, beliefs, and religions. These techniques have been proven useful in reducing the time needed to reach full astral projection. However, it will still take time and patience.

Hypnagogic State

Before mastering any kind of technique for astral projection, you will have to master the hypnagogic state. Hypnagogia is the point between being awake and falling asleep. The transitional state you fall into as the body relaxes, and the conscious mind starts to fade. It is at this point where you might begin to experience hallucinations or lucid thoughts. This is precisely where you want to be. As discussed before, the easiest way to achieve an OBE is through lucid dreaming, placing your body to rest while your mind is still active in a semi-conscious state.

The most common and recognizable phenomena in this state are phosphenes. A phosphene is a phenomenon of seeing light in any shape or form without any light entering the eyes. You can experience this effect now as you are awake as well. Simply close your eyes and place your hands over your eyes without applying pressure to them. This will stop any excess light shining on your eyelids. Now focus, almost as if you are looking into the distance. You might still see some of the after image caused by your screen or any light present in the room beforehand. Simply wait for it to fade out. At this point, you will start seeing the random shapes, patterns, and movements of light without there actually being any.

What makes this the first state to master is not simply the fact that it is the first step to achieving lucid dreaming but also that thought processes in this state can differ significantly from your normal state of mind. It is here where your mind opens up. Where you can see the solution to a problem you could not see before. Your perception of your own ego, of your own reality, crumbles away in this state. Leaving your raw thoughts to be experienced and perceived in a way you might have missed.

Now when we talk about mastering this state, it might be easier said than done for some. But let's try one of the more basic methods of inducing this state, causing you to move on to a lucid dream state.

The best time to start out will be when the body is relaxed and some sleep has already been had. Some people will try to sleep for about 4 to 6 hours and then wake up. You can set an alarm. When awake, do not get up, simply stay relaxed, and observe the dark room, allow your eyelids to slowly close naturally. As you relax, focus on the colors your mind presents you with, they might seem shapeless, but they will soon start to take form. This can take any time between a few seconds to 30 minutes.

Mastering this state means that the shape and forms of color will react to your will in a sense, and you can start constructing your own lucid dream. However, this does take practice, and the chance that you will fall back to sleep without realizing is quite high. In this state, people stumble upon mostly by accident, where they experience their first OBE. Unfortunately, the shock of realizing that you are floating around outside your body is enough to snap you back. Causing you to wake up with a jerking moment, similar to when you fall into a dream.

The Vibrational State

Keeping in mind that you will have to lay completely still. Any itch you might have or twitch you might experience must be ignored to convince yourself that you are, in fact, sleeping. It does help. Okay, so assuming you have done all that and you are entering the hypnagogic state, you will soon start to experience the vibrational state.

The vibrational state is a common state in most astral projection techniques. However, it is not necessarily vibration that you feel, more a sensation of being weightless with a dash of "tinglyness." This state is quite difficult to describe, but you will know when you are there. The feeling can be amplified or lowered merely through willpower. Reaching this state on a first attempt is considered a near-perfect start.

This state is something that can be achieved through basic meditation as well. You can just imagine that if monks dedicate so much time and effort into getting to that point, it must be quite the milestone. Do not be discouraged if you cannot reach it on the first try, or maybe if you do reach it, it slips away very quickly. Mastering this state can be beneficial simply for the fact that you can maintain it. You can convene with your own thoughts in a very clear and profound way, bordering on lucid dreaming while your body rests.

Now, the lucid dream is not our goal here. Our goal is to experience that OBE willingly, and not snapping back to our bodies almost immediately, but instead exploring further and further away. How do we stay outside?

The Rope

After achieving and maintaining the states mentioned earlier, you can start focusing on removing yourself...from yourself.

In school, gym teachers always made you pointlessly climb up those ropes to see who can make it to the top the fastest. Do you remember thinking where the hell you can even apply such a skill? Well, luckily for you, we will be using that skill to get your consciousness out of your body!

Using the rope technique is one of beginners' more popular methods. It is perfect for when lying down in a hypnagogic state. Quite obviously, you will want to be relaxed, being sure that nothing will disturb you will help, so prepare your environment for that. It is preferred to be in a hypnagogic state. It will significantly improve your chances of astral projecting or at least have a quick OBE.

For this to work, you should now be at the vibrational state. At this point, you can start imagining a rope tied to your ceiling, dangling down towards you, just in reach. Not just any rope, this rope has to be detailed. Imagine what the texture is like. Is it moving slightly, or is it completely still? Is it perhaps a heavy chain or rope ladder? These details are mundane. However, they do play a specific role. They make sure you stay focused, visualizing this rope, almost beckoning you to reach out and grab it.

Ok, so you have your rope dangling ready to be grabbed, so? Grab it! Don't physically try and hold it, though. that will not work, for obvious reasons. Visualize yourself lifting your arm and grabbing onto it. Imagine the feel of it in your hand. Visualize placing your arm back next to you and lifting the other one to grab onto the rope. You have to imagine this in extreme detail to keep you focused if you'd like you to start visualizing grabbing onto it with both hands now.

Most people will stop here. Maybe they lost focus, or they actually fell asleep. It's not recommended to try and pull your body up yet, but if you feel comfortable and ready, why not give it a shot? Being your first time, it might not work, but you can keep trying.

So you want to lift yourself up? Great! Visualize lifting both your hands and grabbing on. Remember to imagine it as detailed as possible. Exercise all of your willpower on raising your body up. Starting with your head, then your torso, feeling effortless as you keep going until you leave your body. Now, as I said, this might not work the first time. For some, it does work. However, they quickly become aware of what just happened, and they snap back. The sensation you experience when this does happen is otherworldly. You will know when it does happen.

This technique might not work for you, so why not try a different one?

The Monroe Technique

Robert Monroe was a man well known for his methods and influence on astral projection, specifically in western culture. It helps learn from people with experience, but don't always take it to heart, make your own conclusions, and formulate your own methods. Nonetheless, he documented a specific method that seems to work for most beginners when trying out astral projection dubbed the Monroe Technique.

For this technique, similar to others, you have to be relaxed. As with the rope technique, you have to be in the vibrational state before attempting this technique. It is always good practice to enter and exit the vibrational state even when an astral projection attempt is not on your agenda for the day.

The Monroe technique does not require you to be lying down as he preferred sitting in his favorite chair. It is, however, recommended to beginners to instead be lying down. You can always be sitting somewhere later on when you are used to the practice. Why make it hard on yourself in the beginning.

Okay, so the vibrational state has been achieved. At this point, you can start to increase the state's intensity by enhancing the strange feeling. You can do this by merely focusing on it. While this might feel disorientating at first, imagine what you just did was separate your consciousness from your body. It's still in there—you just kind of need to climb out of your body. Now you can start visualizing lifting a single arm or leg. You are now trying to stand up out of your body, one limb at a time. It does help to have a physical object nearby that you can either try to kick or grab. Visualize this in extreme detail.

This technique is trying to get you used to the sensation of separating from your physical body, slowly but surely.

When you get used to moving your limbs in and out of your body, along with the strange sensation of your current state, you can try and remove yourself completely. This can be done in three different ways. First, you can simply try to stand up out of your body or try and float your way out. Second, you can simply visualize yourself from a third-person perspective in extreme detail. At this point, you will simply be where you are visualizing.

The third is a method similar to the second one. It is usually very successful. Try and imagine yourself above your body. You do not have to face yourself but simply try and feel your physical body right below you sleeping comfortably. This method usually ends up in a quick OBE before snapping back, but it can become quite seamless through mastery. Any technique takes time to perfect, so it is important to practice patience just as much as practicing the method itself.

Did this technique work better for you? If not, don't worry! There are other methods, especially with the technological advancements we have today. Just because this is a spiritual practice does not mean you can't ask for outside or technological help.

Binaural Beats

Some of you may have heard of binaural beats in a different context, perhaps. Binaural beats are, in essence, an illusion. When two auditory frequencies are introduced to the brain through the ears, one frequency on the one side and another frequency on the other, the brain creates a third frequency, a sort of rhythmic beat. These two frequencies are usually very similar but still singularly identifiable for the brain to find the middle ground, so to speak.

These frequencies have been studied in quite a few different ways, with results showing that they can influence the brain positively or negatively, one of the basic examples being the improvement or decline in memory. So what exactly does this have to do with astral projection, you might ask? Well, with research quite limited in this field, I cannot promise anything. However, there are ways this will help, especially if you have trouble relaxing.

In a nutshell, binaural beats can alter the frequency at which your brain is currently operating by changing the way your neurons are firing. This can help by slowing your brain down, in a sense, to get those busy thoughts of yours under control, assisting you with relaxation and sleep. Depending on the frequencies used, binaural beats can get you more focused, change your awareness level, and even alter your state of consciousness. I recommend doing some additional research before considering using binaural beats for any reason, be it for studying, relaxing, sleeping, or astral projection.

Do What Works for You

In the end, these techniques might not be the ones for you. However, they are helpful to beginners. You may interpret them as you wish, use them as you will, and make your own way into the astral plane, do what feels right to you. There are many other methods, and most likely, even more, we have not become aware of yet.

There are a few closing thoughts to always keep in mind when trying this spiritual practice. Firstly, do not become frustrated or discouraged if you are unable to break through. Some people do not have the sense of spirituality others have, similar to how some find the cold more comfortable and others, warmth.

That does not mean you should stop, however. In Buddhism, they believe that it might take many lifetimes to reach enlightenment. Still, every lifetime helps further your inner spirit's energy to become closer to the ultimate goal of breaking free from the cycle.

Secondly, do not let fear guide your thoughts. Nothing can harm you. You are in control. Keeping fear at bay is essential, as it can affect your spiritual journey very negatively.

Thirdly, the ultimate goal for any individual is personal and spiritual growth. These techniques help you reach a point in life where you can make your own perceptions of reality dissipate. To help you interpret reality from a different perspective than you usually would.

FIVE

Developing The Right State of Mind
―――――――――――――――――――――――

WHAT DOES YOUR STATE OF MIND MEAN TO YOU? WHAT DOES having the correct state of mind even mean? Well, I guess that would depend on what you are looking to achieve. The state of mind of a soldier in battle will significantly differ from the state of mind of someone sitting and reading a book.

While our state of mind changes throughout the day, be it voluntary or through circumstance, we can certainly say that whatever state you are currently in will affect the outcome of your task at hand. Now, in the context of astral travel, your state of mind can make your projection process transpire gracefully or stop it from occurring completely in the first place. Let's see how we can change it for the better.

What is Your Current State

These days, many people do not pay attention to their current state of mind; this is prevalent in the statistics surrounding stress alone. So what can you do?

In some behavioral therapy branches, the core of their treatment is by getting the patient to consciously pay attention to what they might be doing. This will influence your mood either for good or bad. This is the same for dialectical therapy, as you have to consciously focus on what you are saying. Okay, so of course, you know what you are saying, but you may not notice how you present your wording, which can subconsciously affect you and the listener.

This is not a great solution, depending on the patient. Someone very anxious might get caught up in their own head and become even more anxious in a social setting. We can look at some basic state of minds, which have been classified as the 6 different states in psychology.

Anxious: As we have just discussed, anxiety can cause quite a crippling state of mind in a social setting. Some people suffer from severe anxiety while merely sitting in their room. Now I am not here to psychologically evaluate you. However, it is crucial to understand the different states in which you can fall. This will help you know yourself better, and in the end, lead to a better projection session.

Anxiety can affect your spiritual journey by causing a lack of concentration on the task at hand. Leaving your mind to wander around, ending with you unable to enter a proper relaxed state. This can be bad for everyday life, but if you want to improve your spiritual practices, you will have to find a way to free yourself from anxiety first. If you feel like this might be you, go see a psychologist or do some research on how to relieve some of that built-up stress and anxiety.

Depressed: Also a very common state of mind, depression sometimes goes undiagnosed and is simply accepted as a temporary emotion of sadness. This can have a highly malevolent effect on your health and cause you to fail at astral projection either completely or cause vivid negative lucid dreaming. No one wants that feeling of having a nightmare and being unable to wake up. In general, depression may cause insomnia, so if you notice yourself becoming a bit more depressed than usual, try and identify the reasons for you to move past it. If you seem unable to do that, find someone who can help.

Anger: Anger is usually a more pronounced state of mind but not always detectable. Some people suffer from great internal anger due to past mistakes or trauma, leading to depression or violent outbursts. Now, comparing what state of mind you want to be in when trying astral projection for the first time to anger, we can immediately see they are quite the opposites. A relaxed, calm, and collected state is tough to attain for people who have a rage building inside. Ironically, this can be their solace.

When anger is experienced, a flood of emotions may take over your mental faculties. Instead of trying to ignore the emotions, you feel at that point, let them come forth. Experience them but do not act upon them. This is a method in which you can let your energy vent instead of building up to the point of no containment. I suffered from fits of rage from a very young age and can confirm that the outburst will subside if you simply let yourself release the energy. After doing that, you will be able to enter a relaxed state. It's almost like a form of meditation, in which you can recollect your thoughts and, rather than react to those feelings, act rationally.

Rational: Speaking of which, this state of mind is considered the perfect middle ground where all parts of the brain are synced in a sense, one not overpowering the other. This does not mean discarding emotion but instead using it as yet another sense. We have grown up surrounded by emotion, some affected by it more than others, some using it to their advantage, and others having difficulty identifying with it. So it makes sense that our brains are, in a sense, trained to detect these emotions in ourselves and others and then use that emotion to find a solution to the current problem or task. You would think this is the perfect emotion to perform astral projection. You aren't entirely wrong, but not completely right either.

Fear: Fear is usually met with a binary decision, yes or no, fight or flight. It is a handy tool in the human arsenal for survival but not very useful when focusing on improving spirituality. Now fear is not simply the primal fear, but also the emotional every day one, the type of fear deep on ourselves's inner side. Trauma or past events, stress, insecurity, doubt, all these things can cause fear inside you. Affecting your very soul, your willpower, your belief that there is something better.

This can obviously affect your astral projection attempt very badly, not just causing your attempt to fail but also a lucid nightmare. The best way to deal with this is usually identifying the origin of the fear. First, meditation can generally be done, but getting outside help is never a bad idea.

Rebellion: A very interesting state of mind from a psychological standpoint, rebelliousness can be very much tied to our childhood, maturing into resentment, anger, and simple stubbornness. This can affect your spiritual journey tragically. Being so caught in your roots, you might not be ready to learn something new, as you will most likely reject it outright.

Some believe rebellion has a great deal to do with our spirits, as we are simply here as humans for a short time. Where did the energy come from, and where exactly it's going after we die, I cannot say for sure. I can confidently say that the energy is there, be it named spirit, soul, or life force. When astral projection takes place for the first time, you start to understand what that energy is, but we are far from comprehending it.

These are the six basic states of mind, which are not the only ones, but the core of what state you might transition to. Astral projection does not require one of these specific states of mind, but rather a state where you are at peace with what is about to transpire.

A state where anger you have felt throughout life dissipated. A state where you have felt betrayed but forgave, where you were depressed but found meaning. You were afraid of change yet had the resolve to think rationally, which can help you realize that there is more to life than what you feel. To what you have known, to what our realities have presented us.

SIX

Influencing Your Astral Body

JUST AS YOU CAN INFLUENCE YOUR PHYSICAL BODY THROUGH what you eat and what you do, so can your astral body be affected by many things. The long-standing popular belief that Buddhists may not eat animals was that they believed it to be unclean. Many people believe today, consuming an animal's flesh will hinder your spiritual progress or even completely halt it.

This is false, however. While there are many variations in Buddhist teachings, not a single one forces you to be vegetarian. The original teachings were more in the line of not making your living off the flesh and death of any living being. What does that tell you? This is a western concept culture sometimes struggles with, as discussed in a previous chapter. Buddhism is not, strictly speaking, religion as western culture classifies it to be. Instead, it is a collection of teachings, which can be interpreted differently from one person to the next.

They do not teach that killing an animal is inherently wrong and so you may not do it. It teaches that animals are alive. They may not be on our level of intelligence or consciousness, but rather that life's simple idea is not to be taken lightly. This will change from the variation of teaching, but at the core of it all lies the sacred idea of life, you, me, your friend, dog, or cat, are alive in this reality. They all perceive this reality differently from you.

To experience reality to the fullest, astral projection is needed, but it is not the whole journey. It is simply a stepping stone. How can we explore further into reality if we are bound by the rules our physical bodies enforce?

There is a method or teaching of life known as Magick, through which you may influence your astral body. The magick believers dubbed it "the science and art of causing change to occur in conformity with Will." Now, to cause a change in conformity means using your own willpower to force change in your reality, the way you perceive life.

In these teachings, it is said that we are simply spiritual energy, occupying these physical bodies. After these bodies die, our conscious energy, our spirits will go one of two ways. Either it is washed of consciousness and repurposed in the cycle of life. Remember, energy cannot be created or destroyed. It can only be changed from one form to the other. So your conscious life force will be used to either provide life to a new human, animal, fire, tree star, anything that requires energy. The second way that consciousness may go would be into your astral body if you prepared it.

The astral body is made out of energy, and your consciousness is a part of that energy. When astral projecting, you project your spirit outward, forming a temporary astral body. Now, what if you can cause a change in conformity through will. Build an astral body, preparing it for yourself after death. At this point, your conscience has something to inhabit should your physical body not carry that burden anymore. This astral body is energy, it cannot be destroyed, so immortality is the result theoretically.

Preparing your astral body may be done in many ways; monks have dedicated time and effort through meditation to dedicate energy to achieve enlightenment. This will then, in turn, fuel the astral body through lifetimes of being recycled until the final point of being able to sustain itself and reach nirvana or true reality. Westerners are mostly impatient, however, and so Magick was born, teaching one to force lifetimes of spiritual progression into one single lifespan.

There are many ways you will be able to influence your astral body. Still, before you can, you will have to develop both spiritually and personally. Knowing yourself better than anyone else is the key to understanding your most inner workings. We dedicate very little time to either because we are too busy, or we are merely afraid of what we might end up finding.

Conclusion

What have you concluded to yourself after reading this book? I can't tell you what you have concluded, you will have to decide for yourself, something we forget we can do, we have a choice, free will and all you know.

I have shown you a small glimpse of historical views on astral projection. I have shown you the small details in different religions that tie them together. I have asked you to have an open mind and break away from your preconceived way of processing reality. I have hopefully answered all of your questions for you surrounding astral projection.

I hope that the techniques we discussed will help you in future endeavors of spiritual and personal growth. I wish you the greatest of luck when trying to improve your mental state, day by day. I applaud your bravery to face change or stand strong in your beliefs. I hope you will further explore what I believe to be an ever-expanding, infinitely, knowledgeable reality.

But before I just leave you hanging, there is one more thing I have to ask of you.

What if?

References

History.com Editors. (2018, August 23). Buddhism. HISTORY. https://www.history.com/topics/religion/buddhism

Radford, B. (2017, October 20). Astral Projection: Just a Mind Trip. Live Science; Live Science. https://www.livescience.com/27978-astral-projection.html

Raypole, C. (2019, July 30). Out-of-Body Experience: What's Really Happening. Healthline. https://www.healthline.com/health/out-of-body-experience

Taibbi, R. (2014, October 31). What's Your State of Mind? Psychology Today. https://www.psychologytoday.com/us/blog/fixing-families/201410/whats-your-state-mind

Turner, R. (n.d.). The Hypnagogic State: How to Have Lucid Dreams Using Hypnagogia. Www.World-of-Lucid-Dreaming.Com. https://www.world-of-lucid-dreaming.com/hypnagogic-state.html

Welcome to Astral Projection Mastery! (n.d.). Astral Projection Mastery. https://astralprojectionmastery.com/

More Books by Monique

Practical Magick
- Wiccan Basics
- Candle Magick
- Wiccan Spells
- Love Spells
- Abundance Spells
- Herb Magick
- Moon Magick
- Creating Your Own Spells
- Gypsy Magic
- Protection Magick
- Celtic Magick
- Shamanic Magick

African Magic
- Hoodoo
- Seven African Powers: The Orishas
- Cooking for the Orishas
- Lucumi: The Ways of Santeria
- Voodoo of Louisiana
- Haitian Vodou

Orishas of Trinidad
Connecting with your Ancestors

The Yoga Collective
Yoga for Beginners
Yoga for Stress
Yoga for Back Pain
Yoga for Weight Loss
Yoga for Flexibility
Yoga for Advanced Beginners
Yoga for Fitness
Yoga for Runners
Yoga for Energy
Yoga for Your Sex Life
Yoga: To Beat Depression and Anxiety
Yoga for Menstruation
Yoga to Detox Your Body
Yoga to Tone Your Body

A Natural Beautiful You
Creating Your Own Body Butter
Creating Your Own Body Scrub
Creating Your Own Body Spray

Last Chance
Join My Newsletter!

If you missed it, I have a free gift available for you and wanted to remind you it's still available.

mojosiedlak.com/self-help-and-yoga-newsletter

Thank you for reading my book.
I really appreciate all your feedback and would love to hear what you have to say! Please leave your review at your favorite retailer!

www.ingramcontent.com/pod-product-compliance
Lightning Source LLC
Chambersburg PA
CBHW071640040426
42452CB00009B/1710